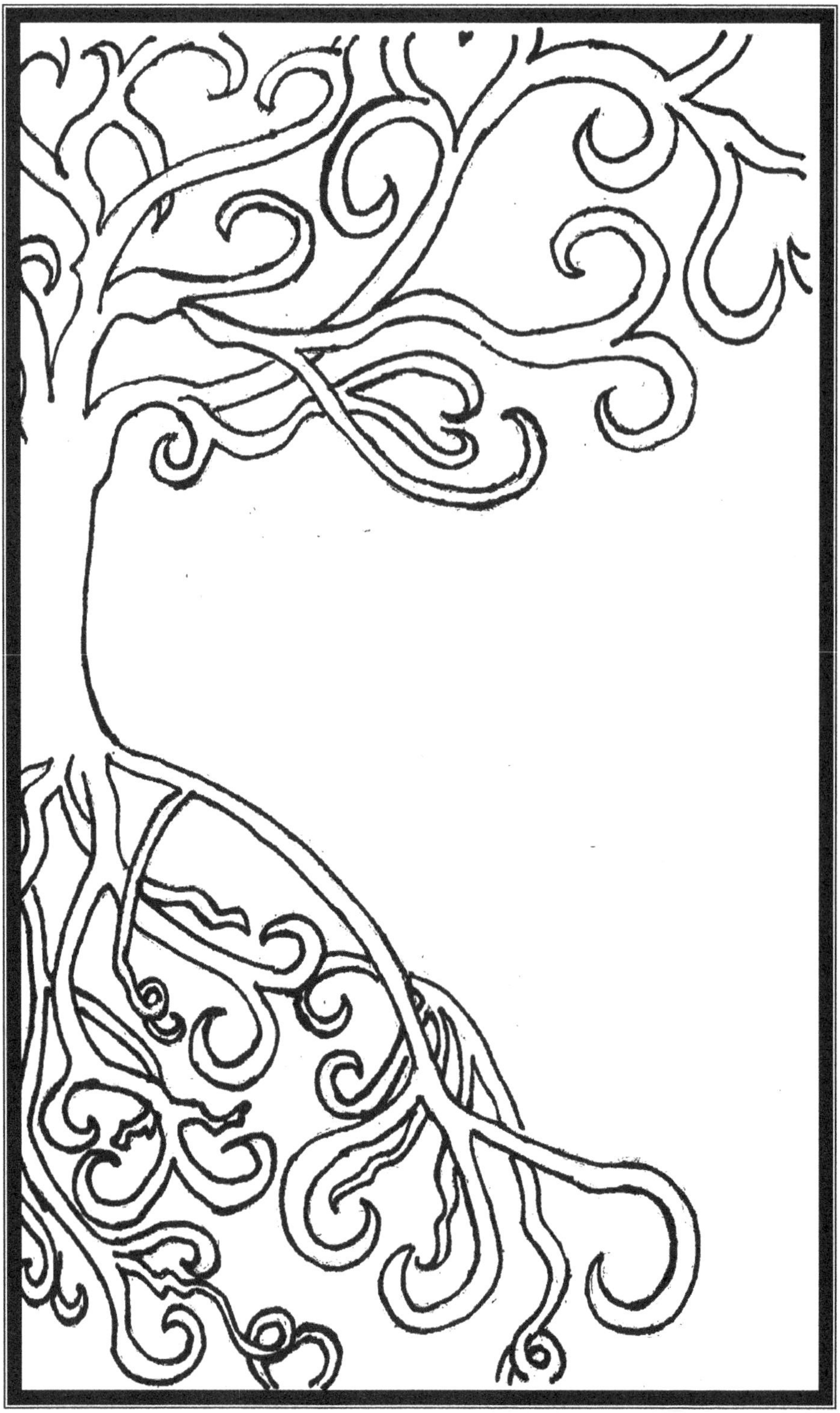

"My Thoughts"
Volume 1
Love

Written By
Emmanuel Ehiemua

Cover Drawn By
Emmanuel Ehiemua

Cover Design By
Emmanuel Ehiemua

Copyright © 2011 Emmanuel Ehiemua
All rights reserved.
ISBN: 1463515863
ISBN-13: 978-1463515867

A Word from the Author

These poems reflect my thoughts about relationships and the ever winding road to true love. Many relationships get caught up in the newness of the *"Chase"* or fall victim to the weariness of the *"Trials"*, never to experience the joy of emotional utopia. Those, passionate enough and strong enough, look forward to weathering the storms in order to see the rainbow and grasp the pot of gold. Dale Carnegie wrote, *"The person who gets the farthest is generally the one who is willing to do and dare. The sure-thing boat never gets far from shore."* To me, true love is an endless cycle that creates and strengthens bonds. An instinctual pull toward the completion of one's very being; comparable to a job and likened to a dream. What does love mean to you? I hope that my poetry encourages you to understand the fundamental phases of relationships, and brings you one step closer to completing your unique love cycle.

Thank you for purchasing my first book of poetry, and please look forward to Volume II, Life.

Emmanuel

DEDICATION

Dedicated to Angel McKee

"Our future was destined to be
Without her there is no me
Our Love has set us free
Thank God for destiny"
-Emmanuel Ehiemua-

CONTENTS

A Word From the Author i
Dedication. ii

Chapter 1   The Beginning

Secret Man......................... p03
Why I Want You.................. p04
Thoughts........................... p07
Sexy................................. p08
I'm Thinking of You............. p11
Dreams p12
Your Smile........................ p15
Sensory Obsession............... p16
Butterflies......................... p19

Chapter 2   The Trials

Destiny............................. p22
Merry-Go-Round................ p25
Rewind............................. p27
I'm Sorry.......................... p28
I Can Feel It In The Air........ p31
I'll Be Waiting.................... p33
Holding On p34
I'll Be There....................... p36
All I Need......................... p38
Together........................... p40
Forgive Me........................ p42
Trust................................ p45

Chapter 3　　Love

Unbreakable……………………..	p49
Krazy Love……………………	p51
Luv………………………..	p53
Love To Love You……….........	p55
I Adore Your Love…………....	p57
What is Love? ………………..	p59
That Love……………………...	p60
One……………………………..	p63
Marriage……………………….	p64

Chapter 1

The Beginning

(The Chase)

Secret Man

Every time I see my secret love, it feels like the first
I hunger for one more glance, to quench my mind's thirst
I've memorized every detail of every inch of her face
When I'm alone, I close my eyes, and begin my mental trace
I trace eyes like almonds with colors that change like moods
Cheeks high and chiseled like Egyptian queens who once ruled
The perfect little nose that twinkles when she grins
The only thing more precious is her perfect little chin
I sketch her lips real slow, admiring while I trace
I kiss the finished product and then marvel at her grace
One day I'll build the courage and tell her who I am
Until that time arrives, I'll gladly be her secret man

Why I Want You

I find it so cute when I look up and it's you I see,
I find it so adorable when you smile at me
You're just the right size for me to hold tight,
You're just the right size for me to love right
I wonder if you catch the thoughts my eyes transmit,
I wonder all day of thoughts I will never forget
Thoughts that are inappropriate but are appropriate just the same,
I want to feel you all over me, like an umbrella feels the rain.
I long to feel your warmth, like opposites that attract,
Your negative seduces my positive; they lock and created the perfect match
I envision us alone under covers of quiet solitude,
Creating and fulfilling fantasies of small and gigantic magnitude

Right now we walk parallel but one day we'll lay perpendicular,
Creating angles of pleasure with degrees non short of spectacular
These thoughts come with haste when I look up and it's you I see,
I have thoughts of you right now, reading this and smiling at me
I wait for the day that I can hold you tight,
I wait for the night when I can love you right
That's why I want you…

Thoughts

I'm having thoughts of you…
Day dreams that run into night schemes of being with you…
My eyes open slowly …And then I exhale…

You consume my mind...
Your touch so soft
Your feel I sought
You're all around me
Calling me
Don't wake me
I'm dreaming…

Sexy

Just thinking of you arouses the hairs on my neck
Just seeing you hardens the passion below my deck
My eyes trace every curve of your hour glass
My nose inhales sweet scents as you walk pass
Your perfect bosom and solid thighs cause my blood to rush
Without thought or array my hands begin to touch
Touching you once is not enough and yields another reaction
Touching you twice, though it feels so nice, only teases my satisfaction
I constantly stand, and hold you close, in silence with physical captions
It's hard to maintain my composure during these warm physical attractions

I think with my head, but not the one, that

receives and processes you

Beyond my control, I'm a slave to the one that

desires to be inside you

It's **S**o overwhelming

Acute but **E**verlasting

Sincere but **X**-rated

Damn, **Y**ou're sexy!

I'm Thinking of You

I really miss your touch

That smile that makes me blush

I really miss, I do,

That silly thing you do

I close my eyes and see, the way you stand and pose,

The way you look at me, before I rub your nose

You're likeable and loveable,

Quite simply just adorable

I'm stuck to you like glue,

I sit and think of you

Dreams

I dream your dream…that dream you dream
So wonderful a dream…a Dream's dream
A dream within a dream, and that Dream dreams of you
Dreaming dreamy dreams of me and you
Good night Dream until we meet again
Close your eyes Dream and dream of your friend.
But in my dreams my friend and I are one,
And we dream the same dreams under the sun
Only a dream but very real it seems
It's very real indeed, but only in my dreams.

Good night….and I love you in my dreams and in my reality,
I love you unconditionally, beyond normality
Is this love? Yeah, it's got to be
Invisible streams of you flow in and out of me
I wish you were here but at least I have my dreams.

I dream your dream…that dream you dream
So wonderful a dream…
A Dream's dream…

Your Smile

Your smile freezes my soul
It captures emotions in ways I didn't know.
I never knew a smile could instantly tame the wild
And cause an adult to feel as a child.
My eyes slightly close and my knees become weak
I begin to stare and lose control of feet.
I quickly look away as my skin becomes flush
Is it normal for an established man to blush?
It's like I sat up too fast and my head began to rush
Your smile makes it hard for me to look but not touch
We've only just met so I guess I'd better hush…
My eyes have already told
Your smile freezes my soul

Sensory Obsession

All I do is think of you…
You completely consume my mind
Your Spirit is imbedded in my senses
In your absence, I feel the absence of time

Your voice is all that I hear…
Sweet tones fill my personal sky
Consonants that vow to address the truth
In your silence, I hear the roar of my demise

Your silhouette is fixed behind my eyes…
A beautiful contour of full resolution
Distinguishing features I will never forget
Homogeneous intensions I will never regret

Exquisite pheromones settle above my lips…
Sensual vapors of appetizing clouds
Delicious fumes that settle on my tongue
Merge taste and smell into the hardness of one

I'm warped in infatuation and I openly stalk your love
I harass your laughs and smiles, and send prayers up above
I'm a slave to your will, without consent or permission
I've diagnosed my condition;
It's sensory obsession

Butterflies

Every time I think of her butterflies form inside,
My lungs swell as I inhale, my lips part to
release the sigh.
My eyes close and a smile is born,
Thoughts are processed and dreams are formed.
My head becomes light and my heart begins to
melt,
I'm submerged in animation from the love I felt.
I awake in surprise, but this always occurs
Every time I think of her…

Chapter 2

The Trials

(Question Marks)

Destiny

Sometimes it's hard to believe in destiny,
And it's hard to see beyond what's in front of me
I know I believe and I know I have the faith,
I just long to catch a break and give happiness a taste
And I long to find the clue that guides me to my path,
And I long for the day to live happily ever af...

I claim to know myself but still I cannot see,
Until it bounces off you and sticks on me
Until I've tried A thru Y, and now I'm down to Z,
And now I'm back where I started, still claiming to know me…

Sometimes it's hard to believe in destiny,
And even harder sometimes to see
But in the end it doesn't matter
Because still I believe…

I believe in you,
And me,
And us

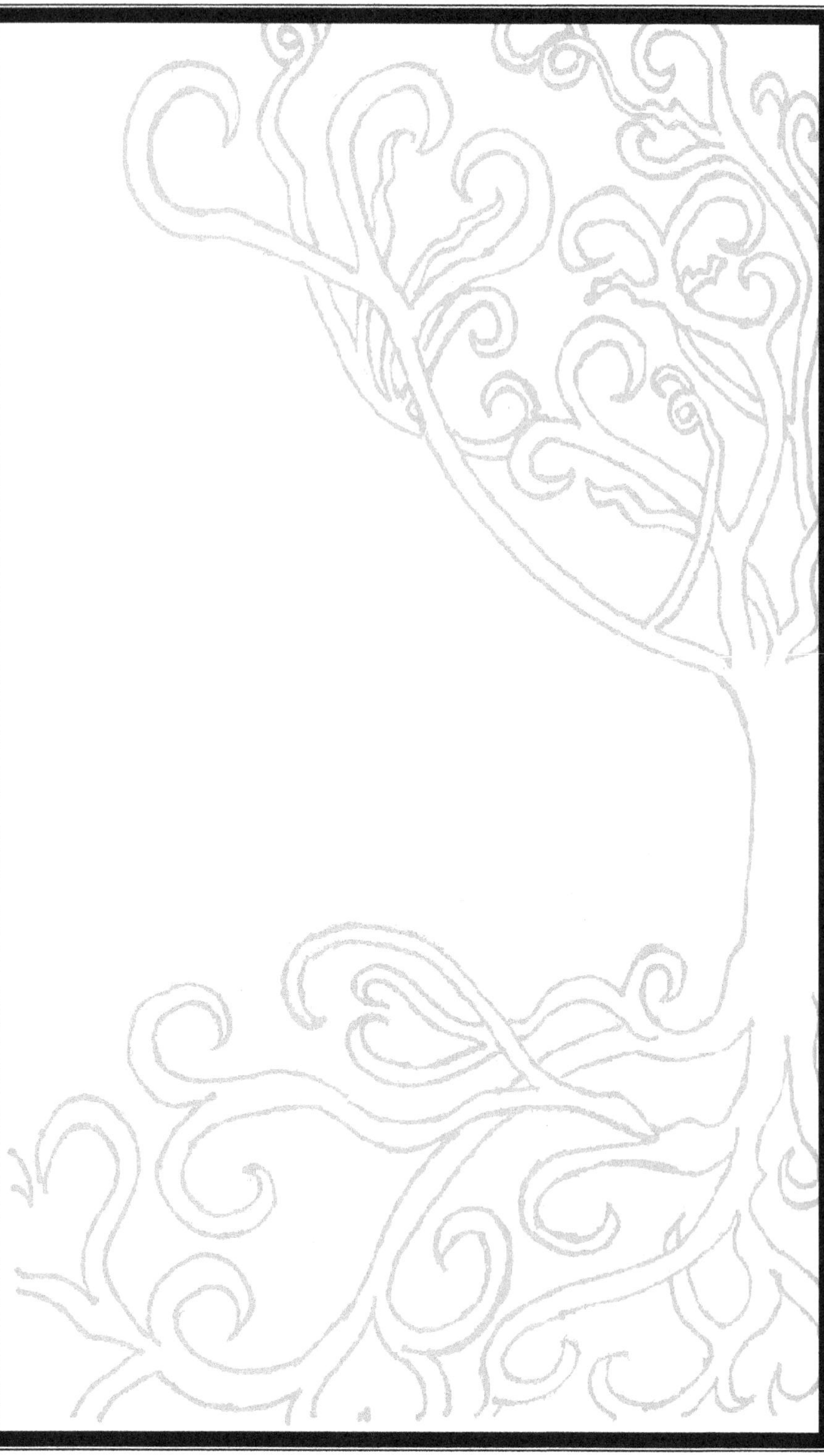

Merry-Go-Round

The tide of life moves up and down but Love
remains unwavering
The "In" and "Out" spins round n' round, that
fact remains unchanging.

Monday thru five felt oh so high, easy smiles,
tender touches and more
Then Saturday came, ya'll at it again, and that's
his reason to walk out the door.

You're too vengeful, he's stubborn as a mule;
Sunday afternoon's more of the same
Make-up sex makes it right and by the end of
the night, ya'll ready to restart this game.

But the "trick-of-the-trade" to longevity is
neither trickery, game nor deceit
Understanding the How and Why the merry-go
-round, can keep Love standing on its feet.

Flow with your tide, ying with your yang, and
diffuse instead of escalating
They say what goes up, must come back down,
but Love is what's left unwavering.

Rewind

I didn't mean to do it,
Shoot my arrow straight through it,
Reel it in and talk to it,
Take hold and control it

I only meant to make it smile,
Whisper sweet nothings and all the while,
Build it up and make it proud,
Dry those tears that filled the Nile

Patch up holes that formed through time,
Smooth out wrinkles and erase all lines,
Sew up halves, if it seemed like two,
Repair the damage that flowed all through

Nurture and mature its very essence,
Love, hug, adore, and caress it,
Merge my own with intended blessings,
Rewrite the past and learn my lessons

I didn't mean to do it; I said that from the start,
I tried to apologize; yet you listened not,
It's just our fate that we must now part,
I again apologize for breaking your heart,

If I could, I would rewind time....

I'm Sorry

I'm sorry for the way I've been,
I'm sorry I haven't spoken to you as a friend.
I'm sorry I haven't treated you as a mate,
I'm sorry I haven't been acting so great.
I'm sorry I haven't shown you that you're my love,
I'm sorry for causing our tempers to rub.
I'm sorry for causing you to walk out my door
I'm sorry for forgetting who I have feelings for.
I'm sorry for forgetting and always losing sight,
I'm sorry from within and I hope to make this right.
I'm hoping you can forgive a spoiled young man,
I know you have before, but I hope once more.
Once more for you to see past my arrogance,
And realize that I would crumble in your absence.
I know the world would be cold if I couldn't feel your presence,
I wouldn't know how to be a man if it wasn't for your reference.
It was you, who first taught me how to grow up,
You again, who showed me paths when times were rough.
It was you who made me see my pig headedness,
You again, who took me by the horns during my bullheadedness.

It was you, who showed me that lovers can be friends,
My only pure angel in my life of sin.
The voice of reason, when it's red I see,
When it seems that the whole world is at war with me.
I don't know what I'd do without you by my side,
It would be like standing at happiness' gate with no key to get inside.
Like chasing a lost love down an endless street,
Like gasping for air after my heart skips a beat.
I'm sorry for the way that I have been
I can't swear to God, but I hope never to do it again.
I'm sorry…

I Can Feel It in the Air

I know right now things between us aren't the same
I'm reminded of what happened, every time you say my name
As I search inside for shelter from the rain
You search inside too, for a way to ease the pain
This is all new to me; I've never been here before
I've always been the one to close the door
I've always been the one to cause heartache
I knew I'd feel the karma for the choices I make
I still live by the phrase of, "What Will Be Will Be"
So I'll keep hope for you, if you keep hope for me
I haven't blocked the path that leads to our wedding day
This obstacle just means we'll take the long way
After the tears dry up and our hearts begin to repair
I think we'll be alright, I can feel it in the air

I'll Be Waiting...

I'll be waiting for you, holding my breath
Standing in salute until I have nothing left
Counting each minute until your return
First and second guessing when you'll be by my side
Holding hands together, we'll float through life's ride
Sharing souls forever as we look to the stars
Separate, we'll never, we love therefore we are
I'll be waiting for you...

Holding On...

I'll keep holding on, no matter the situation
I feel we are meant to be despite negative persuasion
I don't care about barriers, restraints, or walls
I see through the haters and ignore them all
I know what I did then, but this is the now
But if "Then" plagues your mind, I'll fix it somehow
I don't have all the answers but I plan to make a plan
I'm not running from my destiny, I plan to take a stand
I don't care if no one else can see what I see
All that matters is your eyes and how they choose to see me
Not a soul can break us, except for our own
Imagine coming in from work with no me in your home
We often cuddle while we sleep, so the past has shown
Imagine turning to your left but only I'm gone...

What you're feeling right this second, I've felt it too
Only once before, at the thought of loosing you
It's a strange type of feeling, one you can't explain
Before love, I never understood the power in a name
Before you, I never really believed in soul mates

I never starred at anyone and smiled just for smiles sake
I never thought I'd find someone who's just as silly as me
Someone who's real throughout, just like me
Someone who senses feelings, just like me
Someone who sees me, the way I see me
Only now, when I see me, I see you
Now "One" means both of us, it's no longer us "Two"
So I could never let go, because I'd be incomplete
Without my better half, what kind of person would I be?
It'll be just us "One" until our child is born
No matter the situation, I'll keep holding on

I'll be there

Whatever comes your way, I will be there for you.
When you're at your lowest point, I'll stand tall for you
When you're at your peak of bliss, I'll rejoice with you
When there is fire in your eyes, I'll never lose cool
When you are carrying heavy loads, I will share them with you
And when you need to be alone, I can handle that too
When you need my full attention, it'll be just us two
No shows, no games, no family, no crew
No phones, no work, no me, just you
Just ears wide open and lips shut for you
When you need my protection, I'll be there for you
If I had to choose, I would compromise for you

If you get bored with "us", I'll fix that boo
We'll meet again for the first time and start anew
There will never be a limit for what I would do
Rain, sleet, or snow too…I'll be there for you

All I Need

All I need is you, to make it through today
Your elegance paves my mind and shows me
the way.
All I need is you, to make it through tonight
Warm embraces from you to me, right all
wrongs and set me free.
All I need is you, to get through this week
Your smile gives me strength when this world
has made me weak.
All I need is you, to make it through the month
Your stroke can seize my frown and turn it
upside down.
All I hope for is you, to make it through the year
One kiss on New Year's Eve, eases fear and
makes me believe.

Without your presence and your love, I'd
crumple at the start.
Restless days and sleepless nights,
Troubled weeks and monthly fights

Painful years of unproductivity,
Wishing for wishes to find you next to me
I don't want to feel that pain, or trouble, or fright,
So right here and right now, I've made the choice to treat you right.
I've made the choice right now, to always do my best,
I promise to do my best and let love handle the rest
And if "promise" and "love" fail to keep trouble back,
I'll fall to my knees and pray "He" has my back…
Without you, there is no me….

Together

Sometimes we complain about the do's and don'ts
And arguments are created out of anger and taunts
Sometimes it's hard to separate our needs and wants
And tension is formed that can last for months
Sometimes we forget that there is no "I" in "Team"
And while trying to be the star, we lose sight of the dream
Sometimes we ignore the rainbow and only see the green
And it all becomes gray, because that's the way it seems
And it all seems lost because that's the way you feel
Like no one gives a damn because it's not their deal
Like commitment and fidelity are ideas of the past

Like respect and gratitude are going no where fast
Just pause….
Take a moment and a breath
Count to ten if you must and forget about the rest
Close your eyes and exhale so the stress may be released
Take another breath to fill your heart and soul with peace
Then remember your friends, family, and mate
Then consider the way, they might have spent their day
Have you argued with her or screamed at him?
Have you ignored their calls or acknowledged them at all?
Try not to forget, there is no "I" in "Team"
If she's truly your soul mate, then you share the same dream
If he's truly your heart, your soul, and your air
Flush away your animosity and leave it there
No person has the power to predict the weather
But trust in God, and in love, and you can face it forever,
Together…

Forgive Me

Bear with me…
I'm closer to my dream
Forgive me
I know it sometimes seems
That I am distant
But my heart is always near
So bear with me
And erase all fear

Try to see…
My heart is in the right place
Believe me
It's all over my face
I love you
And I could never do without
So bear with me
And erase all doubt

Forgive me…
I know not what I do
When I am angry
It's me and never you
I cherish
Every day that I have you
I'm embarrassed
For every second hurting you

I promise…
For every promise I have made
I swear
Under God and today

I'll try
From this moment and you'll see
I'll try even harder to be a new me

Please
Bear with me…
Try to see…
Believe in me…
Forgive me…

I'm sorry

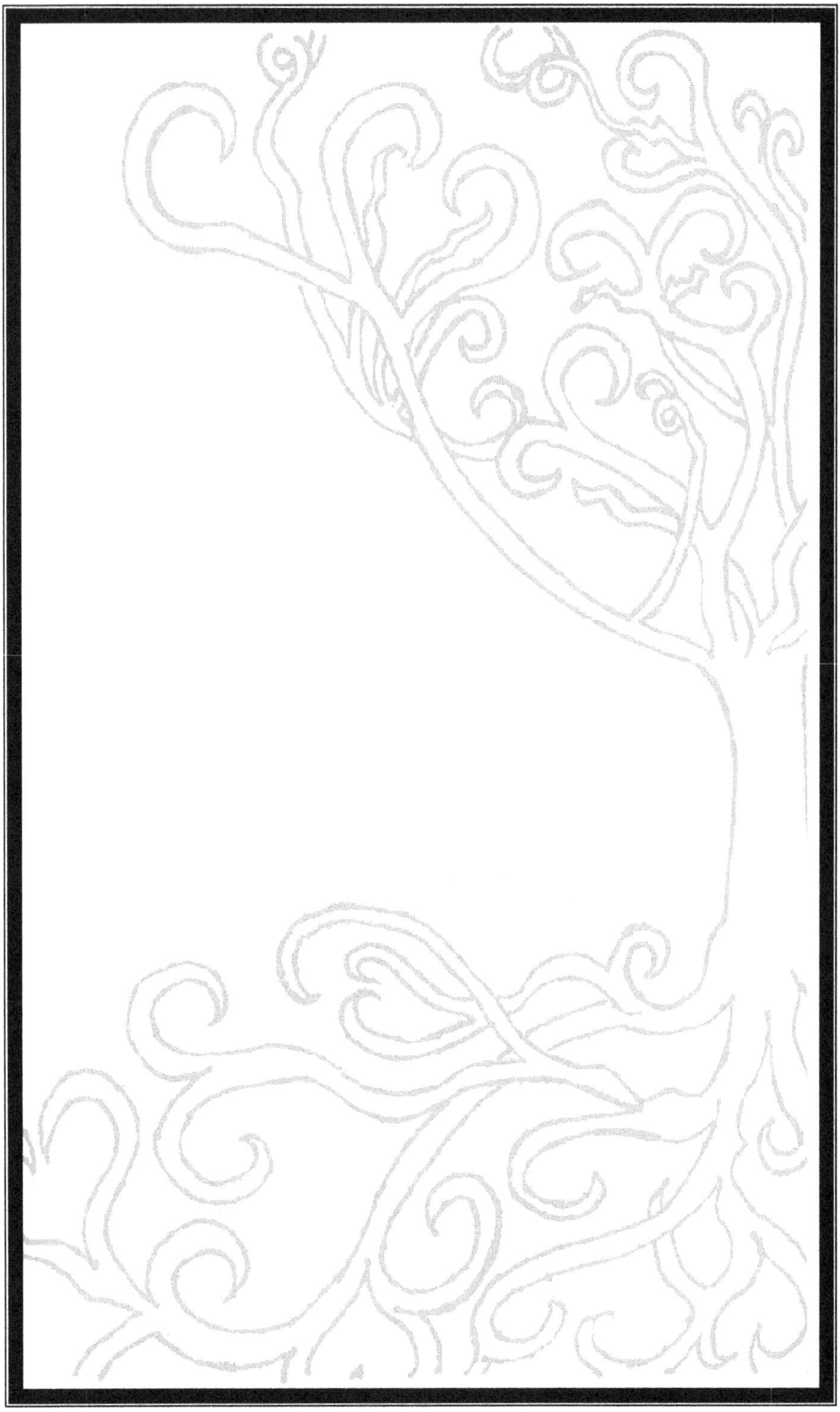

TRUST

Trust…the hardest of those things
Those things that one must have; to help Love grow and last
Faith… that bare essential thing
That leap toward true meaning; that dream of rings and things

Those two are tough to bare, hard to swallow and difficult to grasp
It's so easy to let them be when times are dire and tempers clash,

But then there's…,

Love…that's why you both are here
True Love will stand the test; tough times just mold the best
And your heart must know no fear, for the fear just breeds despair
Step through the looking glass, and grab your happiness at last,

But back to…,

Trust…so easy way back when
There was no fault or sin; no one could lose or win
But your heart must know no fear, for the fear just breeds despair
If this Love was meant to be, this will not stop it; you must believe,

But can you…,
Trust

Chapter 3

Love

(Fidelity)

Unbreakable

Our bond grows stronger with each day
With feelings that are untamed in trend and nearly impossible to envision
With a love that is emergent and overlapping in dimensions
With thoughts that are collective even when conjured discretely
With actions that are harmonized in fluency and potency
With words that are synchronized in rigidness and integrity
With an understanding that is singular, curious, and unique
With a closeness poured into a mold of perfect physique
Our bond is unmistakable
Precious and irreplaceable
Invisible but perceptible
Inescapable
Unbreakable

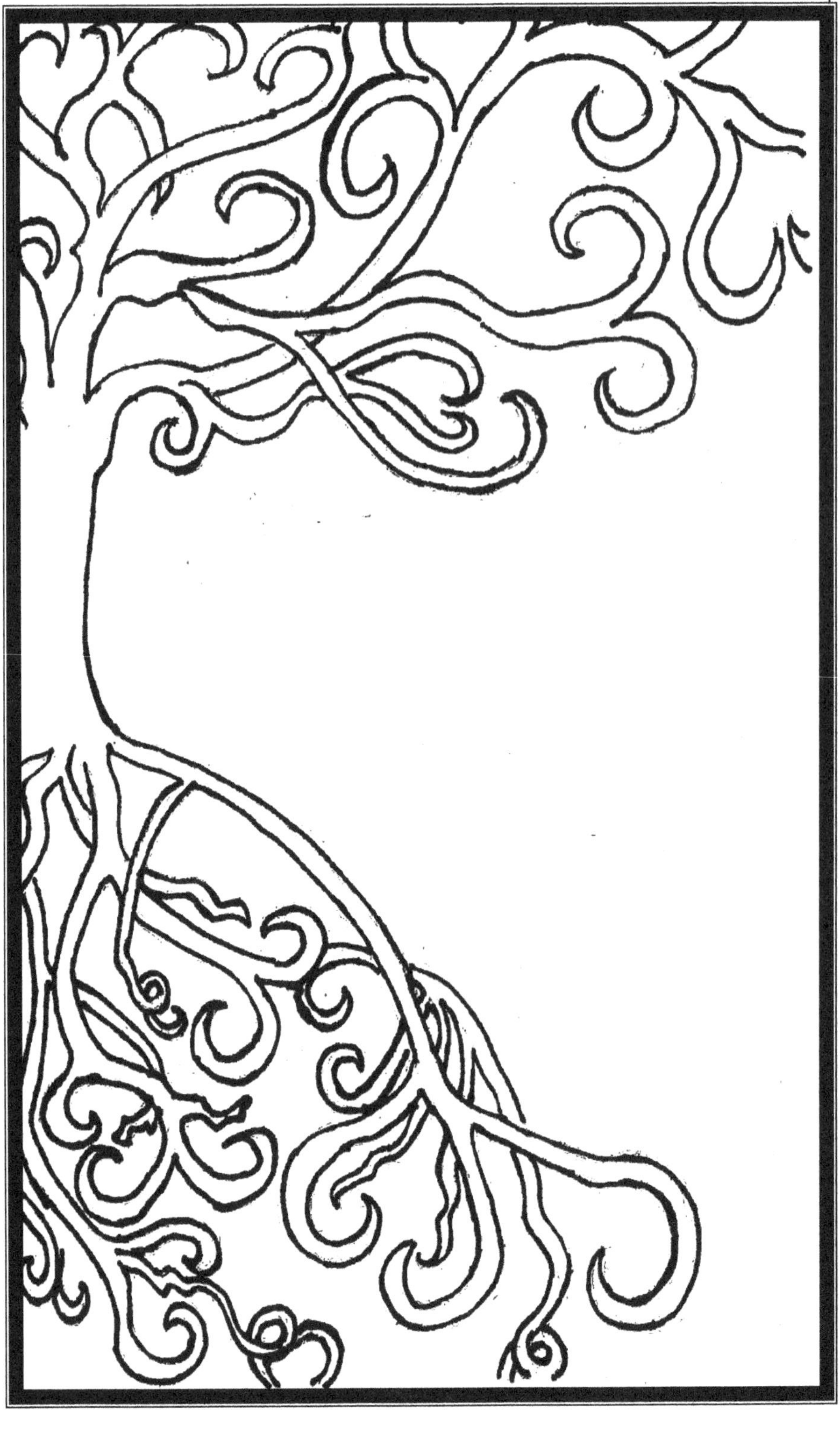

Krazy Love

I'm dizzy,
Head Spinnin
Mind runnin
Stomach turnin

I'm weak,
Knees numbin
Eyes shunnin
Heart thumpin

I feel warm,
Blood rushin
Sweat gushin
Breath hushes

That daze from Above
It's Krazy Love…

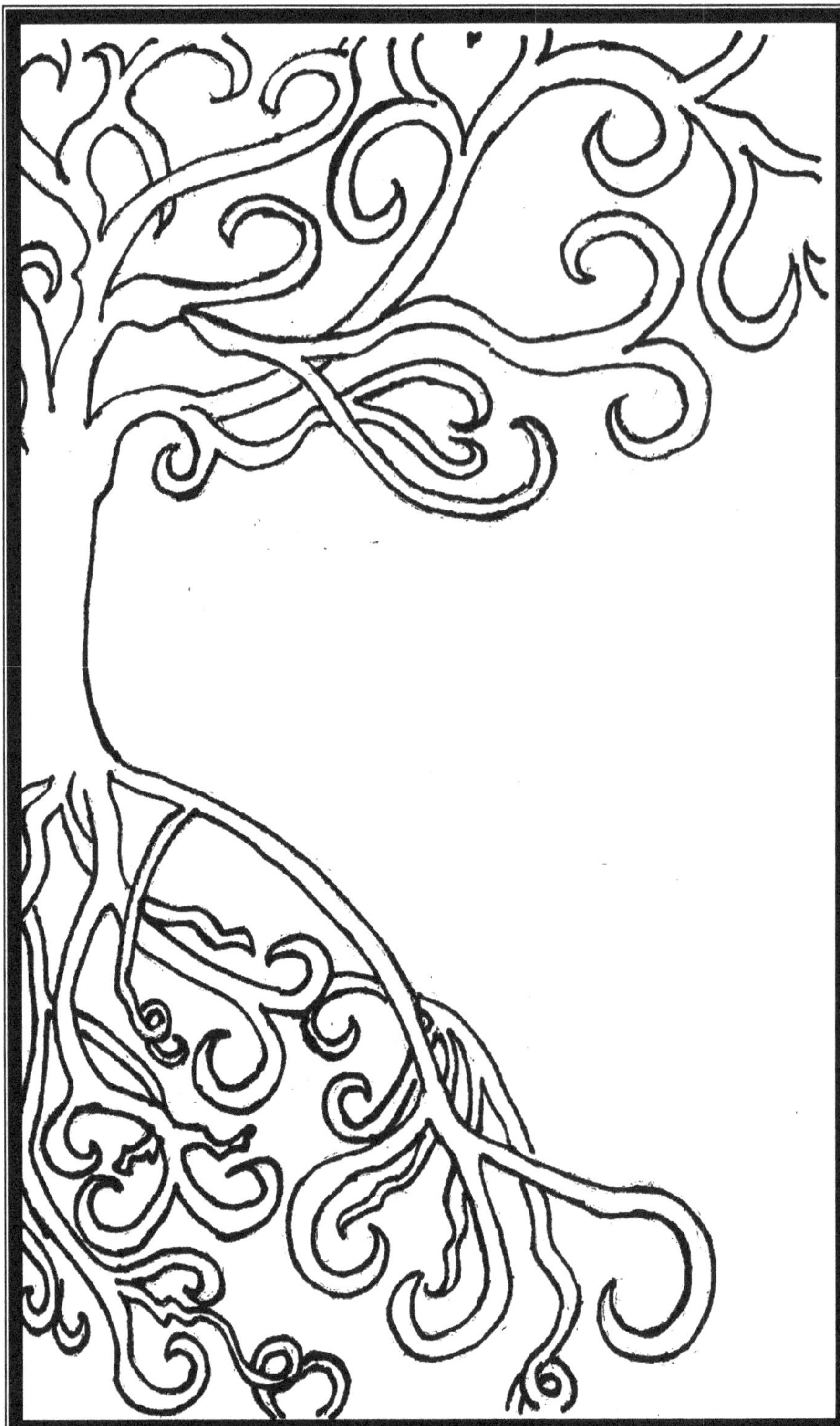

Luv

Sometimes you're slow to bed and early to wake up
Sometimes you're spent, like you don't give a fuck...

Excuse my French, but you know what I mean
When her smile is heaven, when his touch is a dream
But when his arrogance is vile, and when she irks for miles
But then you make up...yeeaahh, you make up...

Sometimes you rush to get home and on to the moan
Sometimes you long to be alone ...

Excuse my candor, but you know how it is
When you're lost in her spell, when you're aroused from his smell
But when he loses his temper, and when she crosses that line
You don't give up...nah, you *won't* give up...

Cause he's always right on time, and she's still your dime
The treasure chest that holds your key,
Even if today is gone, tomorrow's at dawn
Sounds a bit much,
But such,
Is Luv

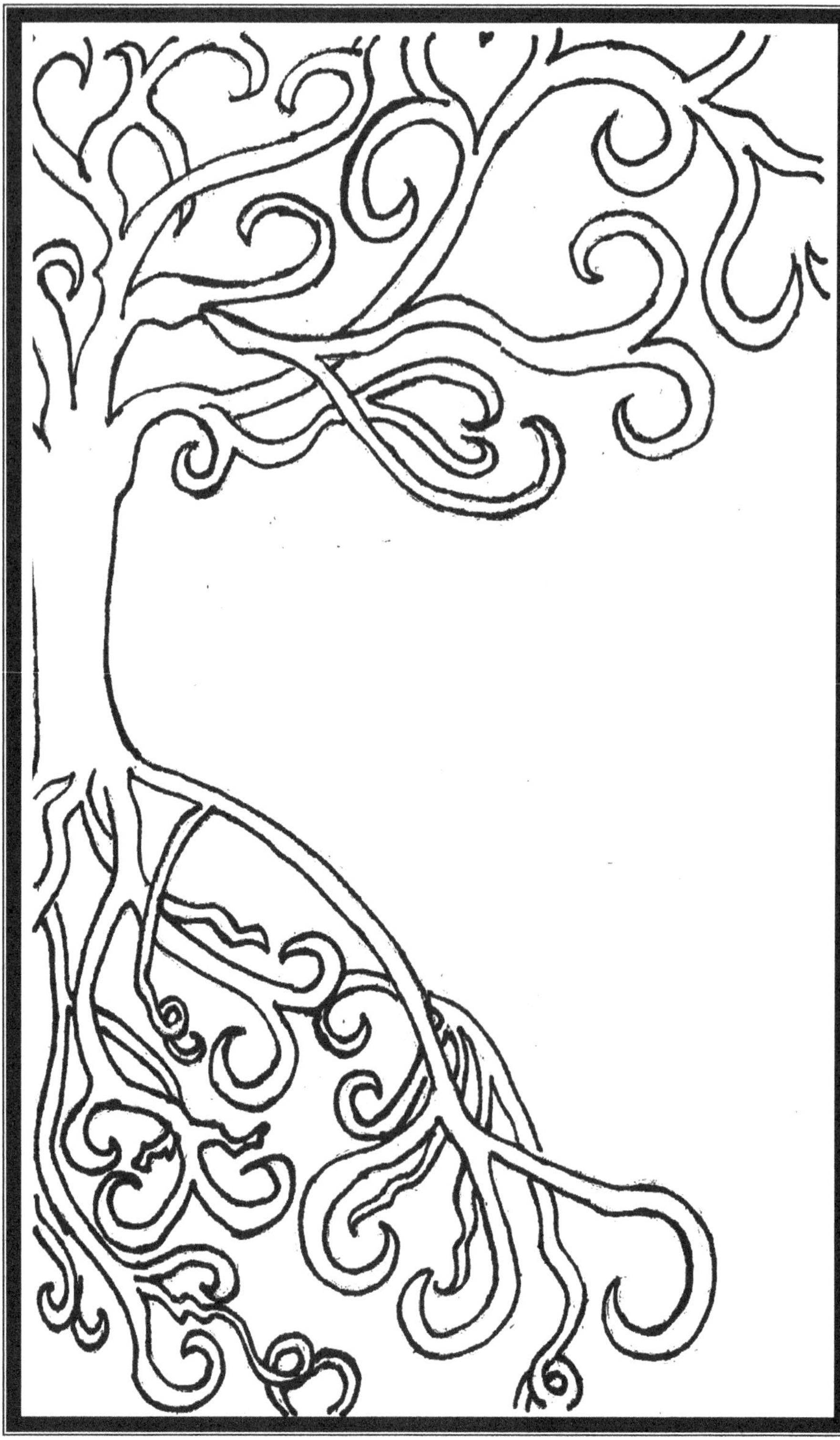

Love to Love You

I love loving you…
The way you smile from ear to ear,
The twinkle in your eyes when I am near
The radiant curves of your lips,
The sexy flow of your hips
I don't know much but one things true,
I really love loving you

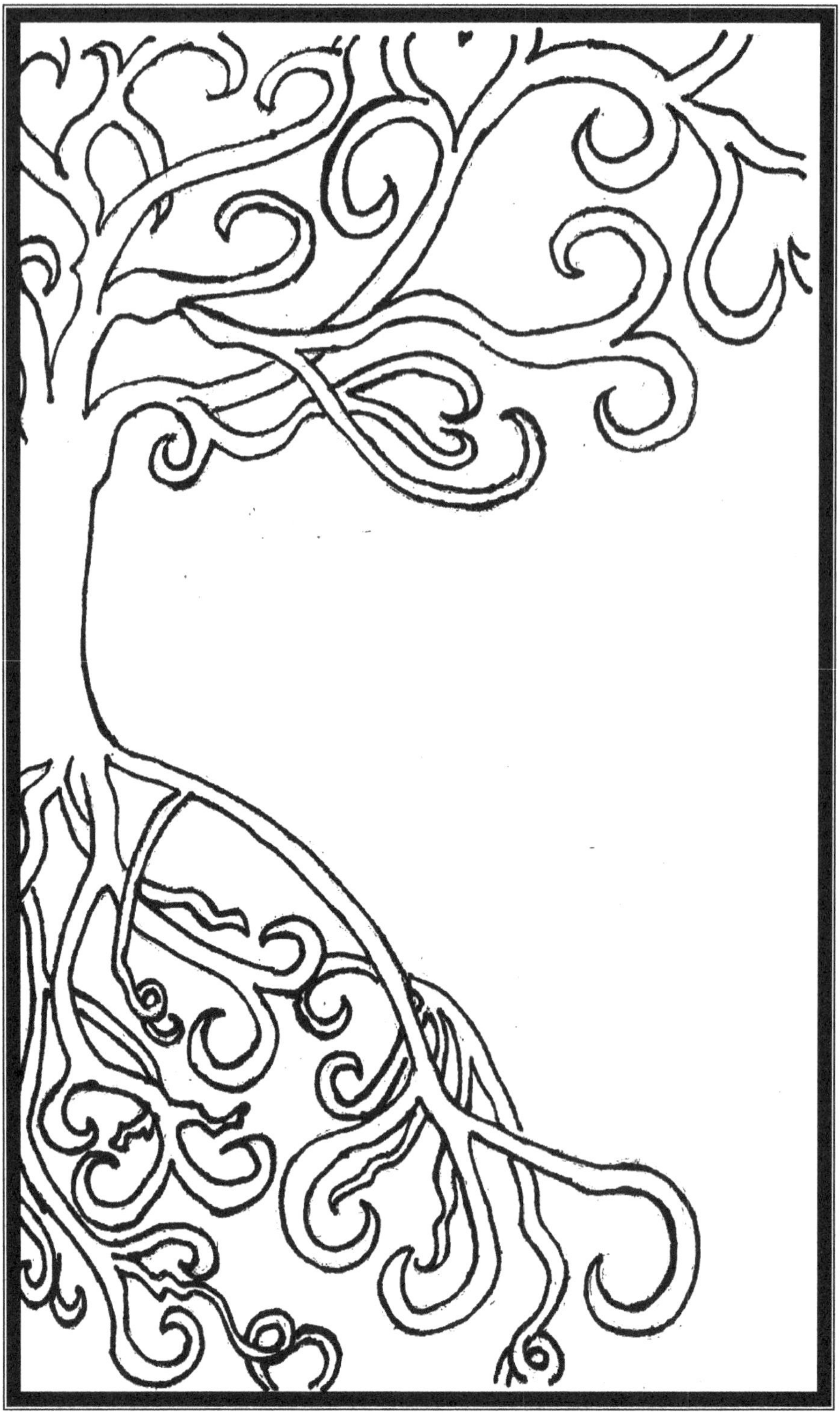

I Adore Your Love *(Ton Amour)*

I adore your love
Your love I adore
Ton amour es mi amor
Mi amor, ton amour
Precious treasures hidden in a chest with no lock
Inner roses wither... She loves me, she loves me not
I think she loves me, Can I count the ways?
So strange is our love, A labyrinth's maze
So difficult I make it but secretly provide paths
Yellow brick roads and words untold point to where I'm at
My chest swells as I wait to inhale
Anxiety and light headiness fill my well
I release winds of change and embrace the eye of the storm
Where before rained chaos, now rest only calm
I adore your love
Your love I adore
Ton amour es mi amor
Mi encanta, ton amour

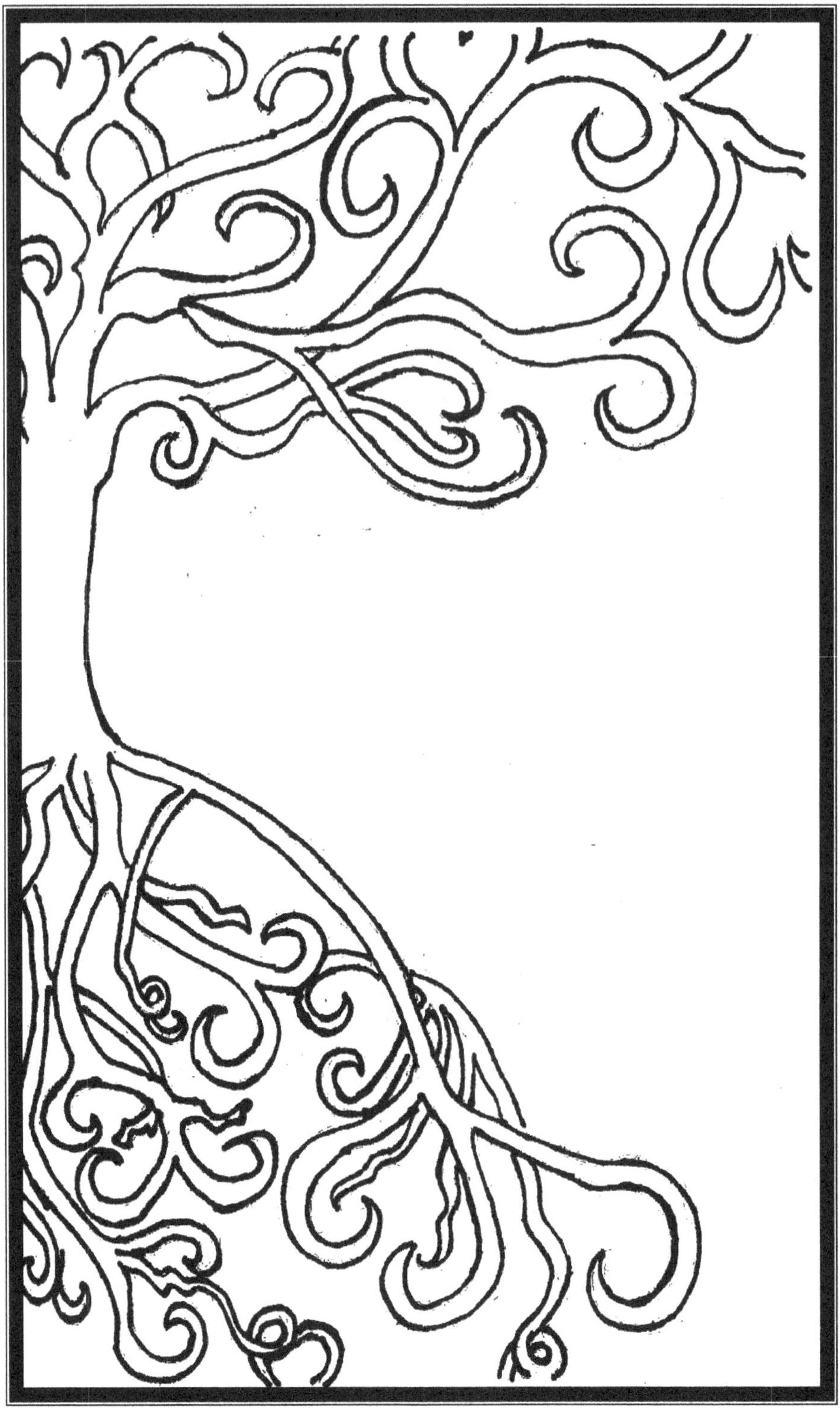

What is Love?

Love….So what does that word mean to you?
A rose, a clue, the essence of the true
A bridge from me to you;
The Perfect ….
The everything you've ever wanted
You'd wear it abreast; yeah you'd flaunt it…

But it aint all peaches and cream, some times are rough;
Sometimes you question, Is it just enough?
But I digress …
This here is for That
That which keeps you here;
That which crystal clear is the Love

What does Love mean to you?
A rose, the true, the best part of you
The Perfect….

That Love

It's been awhile, but never the less,
I am still filled with that Love
That feel; that smell, eyes lost in her spell,
That Love…!
And My Heart is Overjoyed, to the limit it grows
Still weakened by her charm, curls down to toenails
That hug; that kiss, We're lost in our bliss,
That Love…!

So I'm here writing this, or so it seems,
A familiarity, tongue twisters, and such
It's beautiful or wonderful; what ever you fancy,
What else can I say about That Love…!
And oh how the pen glides, while words align
Which ones are worthy to be chosen?
Splendor, grandeur, magnificence; sumptuousness,
Synonyms that lionize That Love…!

Still laymen's will do, for exuberance is a given
And popularity is never a necessity
Just a cup of our essence and 3 quarts of His blessings
It makes sense when you know about
That Love...!

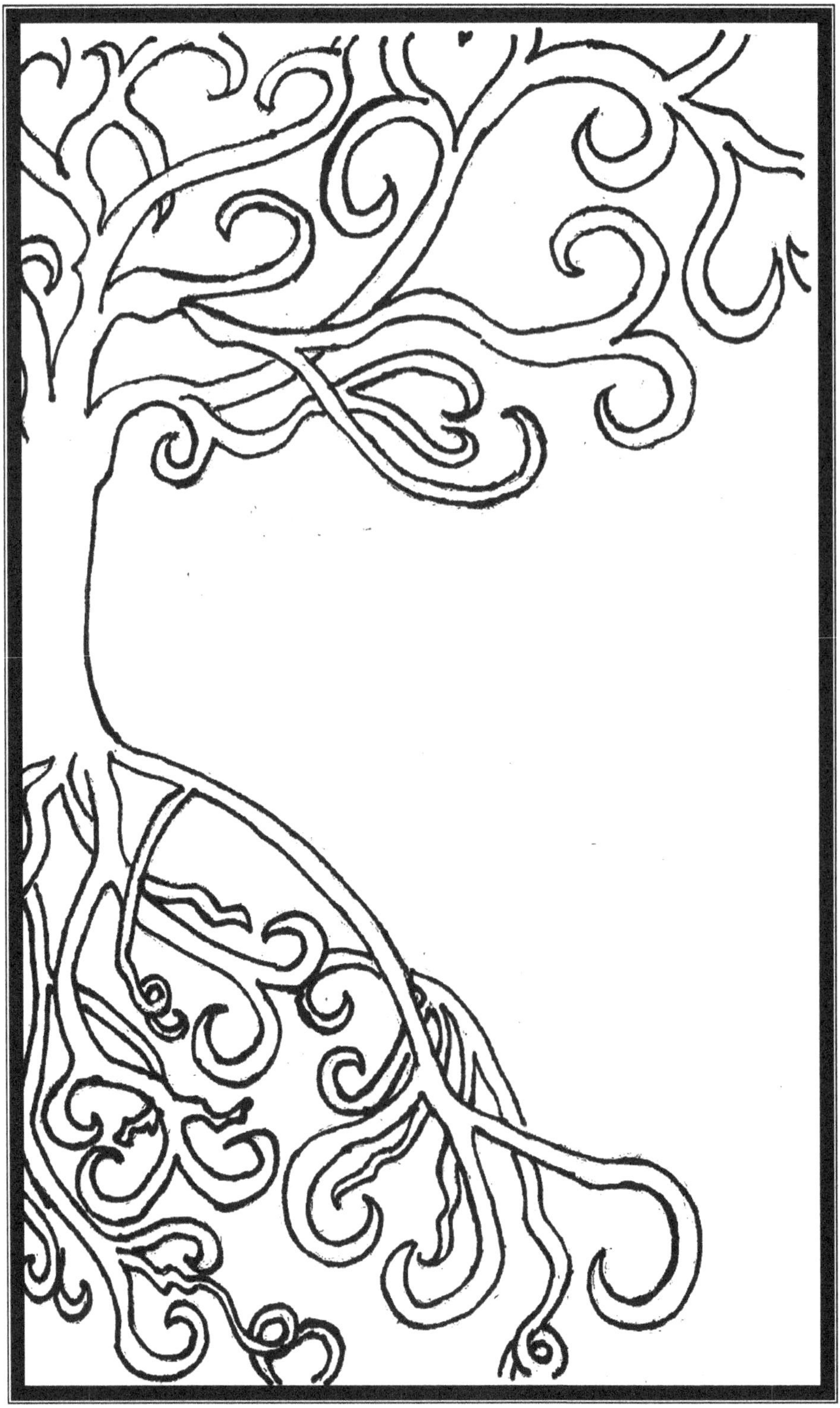

One

Our souls are attached…
And though you might not agree that you are a
part of me, I cry your tears…
I see through your eyes and you hear through
my ears...
Apart we are cold…
Together we are one mind, one body, one heart,
and one soul.....
Forever us

Marriage

Defined as the union between two things
The joining in wedlock of a Queen and a King
The legal union of a daughter and a son
The merger of two hearts and two souls into one

Our love is so much more, I wish you could see
Invisible streams of her, flow through me
The essence of what is me, lives in her
If you could only see our light, you would concur

A light that is pure and everlasting till the end
A light that will shine through darkness or sin
A light that is evident on earth and the spiritual realm
A union of happiness, confirmed and blessed by Him

Happiness within that has always remained innate

A happiness of the soul unlocked by a soul mate
A joy of the spirit uncovered by a best friend
The emergence of a love, reborn again and again

Everyday is like brand new, I wish you could see
The unbreakable bond between her and me
We've begun our passage, only one thing to do
That's pledge our love under Him and before you

Can you see…..?

Made in the USA
Columbia, SC
07 October 2022